Search Engine Optimization

Simplified

7 Steps plan for SEO

By

Subodh Gupta

Corporate Trainer & SEO Consultant

First Edition July 2008

ISBN 978-0-9556882-8-7

Published by
Subodh Gupta
+44(0)7966275913
Head office: London (UK)
Email: info@subodhgupta.co.uk
www.subodhgupta.co.uk

This book is available for special discounts on bulk purchases. Please contact at the publisher email address or phone number.

Publisher Note:

Acknowledgements

I am grateful to my parents and all my teachers who taught me at various stages of my life & shared with me their wisdom.

Content

Part 1: Understanding SEO terminology

Part 2: 7 Steps for Search Engine Optimization

Part 3: Recording and measurement

Introduction

This book is based on my 3 years of research on working of the search engines.

If followed correctly, this book will help you to achieve an envious presence on most of the major search engines. This book does not contain any magic trick rather I would call them as practical and effective approach to get you there where you would love to be.

Nowadays in business, search engine is the first place where people turn towards whenever they have to look for any information. So a good ranking on search engine is certainly a must otherwise you may end up losing many customers to your competitor.

In this book, I have tried to explain the search engine optimization in a simplified way so that you can improve the ranking of your website.

If you work consistently and correctly, you should start seeing results within 4 to 5 weeks time and can see significantly improvement in your website ranking within 9 to 14 weeks time.

Even if you decide to outsource your SEO work to some other company, I would suggest that still it is good to know the SEO process as it will help you to manage the SEO company in a better way as some time SEO consultant use unethical practices to improve the ranking of their clients website which when caught by search engine can leads to banning of the website from the search engines results.

The algorithm of search engines (by which search engine determine the rank of a website) is keep changing and because of that lot of SEO consultant worry a lot however there are some aspects which are essential for good user experience and they are not going to change much for the long time to come. So the most important step to begin the SEO process is to focus your mind on your user rather than the search engines.

When you build your website keeping your user in your mind considering what he will needs, like and want, you are already on your way for achieving good ranking for your website in search engine results.

Now along with keeping your mind focussed on your user there are 7 main steps for SEO which I have explained in this book and I think you needs to consider them while building your web site.

This book is divided into 3 parts. Part 1 explains various terms which are used in reference to the search engine. Part 2 explains seven action points step by step which will help you to optimise your website and improve its ranking in the search engine results. Part 3 is about recording and measuring the improvement in the rank of your website in the search results.

I wish you all the best and I hope this book will give you insight into the world of search engine.

With Best Regards

Subodh Gupta

Part 1

Understanding SEO Terms

What is a Search engine?

Search engine in the simplest term can be defined as a web page where the users can search the information on the World Wide Web.

User can type the keywords and he can get the relevant information in the form of web pages or images. Popular examples of search engines are Google, Yahoo etc.

Globally Google is the most popular search engine at the moment i.e. having maximum visitors from all over the world.

However on regional basis in some of the countries few local search engines are more dominant than Google.

For example in Russia local search engine **Yandex** is more dominant than Google and similarly in China **Baidu** continues to lead over Google.

Should I submit my website to all the search engines?

You may come across various emails from search engine consultants who will explain you that for a certain fee they will submit your website to thousands of search engines.

Although you can submit your site to hundreds or thousands of other search engines however time and money spent in submitting your site to other search engines may not be justified.

In my personal opinion unless your customer is based in China and Russia (where you to focus on regional search engine as well), you need to mainly focus on Google (as it has the largest share of customers all over the globe) and you would find that your website is doing well in all the other major search engines like Yahoo, MSN, etc. of its own, i.e. you don't have to pay extra or spent extra time for registering to hundreds of other small search engines.

What is Search engine optimization?

Technically saying the term search engine optimization is incorrect as it is not the search engine which is optimises rather we optimise our website so that it can rank higher in search engine results.

Many entrepreneurs and organizations launch their website with beautiful designs and lots of content but without really understanding that how the search engine work and what it needs.

For optimizing your website you need the understood what factors search engine use in order to rank a website.

Although according to Google they use more than 100 factors for ranking a website on search engine results however if you provide essential aspects which are must for good user experience and search engine requirements, I am sure you can see a great improvement in the ranking of your website. Also these essentials factors would keep your website ranking relatively safe when search engine algorithm changes.

Now without going into technical stuff, Search engine optimization (SEO) can be defined as the process by which one can increase the volume and quality of traffic to one's web site from search engines (like Google, Yahoo etc) via "natural" or "organic" search results by improving the ranking of one's website.

In general the higher the rank of your website on the search engine results the more traffic or visitor you can get from the search engines.

What SEO (Search Engine Optimization) involves?

SEO may involve editing website content, simple coding, developing useful content for consumer, identifying and focussing on relevant keywords, adding sitemap, correcting the HTML title of the various pages on website, structure, as well as fixing problems that could prevent search engine from indexing the pages of a website in its search, etc.

Algorithm

An algorithm is a sequence of instructions or set of instruction for calculation and solving a problem.

It can also be defined as a procedure for completing a task through a well defined instruction.

Let's understand it with the help of an example;

Let's say you type a keyword **"holiday"** in the Google search engine and press **enter** on your keyboard.

Within a fraction of a second you get the following results:

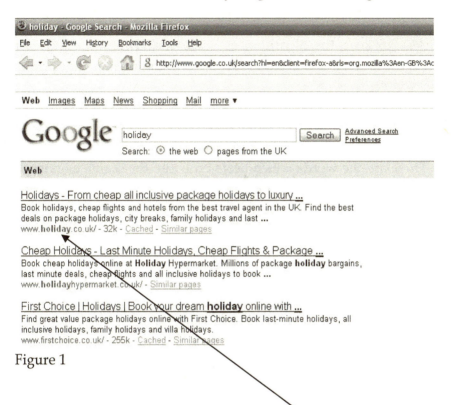

Figure 1

Now the ranking of the website www.holiday.co.uk (shown above) and all other subsequent website below it depends upon Google algorithm. So as this website is ranked at number 1 position on page 1, it will get the maximum visitors because of its position and hence expected to earn maximum revenue.

Since revenue of most of the websites depends upon their ranking on search results, which is determined by the algorithm of search engines i.e. everybody wants to figure out the algorithm of search engine. This is one of the major reasons that the exact algorithm of search engines is a closely guarded secret as otherwise people can always manipulate that.

Also to keep the algorithm as a secret and improve the user experience, the search engine keeps on updating their algorithm.

Keywords

These are the words which users type into the search engines to get the relevant information.

For example in figure 1; "**holiday**" is the keyword which is typed in the Google search bar.

Keyword Density

It is the percentage of targeted keyword upon the total text on a webpage.

Suppose a webpage which is targeted for a particular keyword such as "holiday" has total number of word (text) on the page equal to 200 and the word "holiday" has been mentioned on the page by 10 times; then the keyword density of "holiday" word on this particular page will be 10 divided by 200, equal to 5%.

Keyword Stuffing

Excessive use of keywords (keyword repeatedly used) on a webpage either as a text or as hidden HTML elements in Page title, or Meta tags.

Meta elements

Meta elements are HTML or XHTML elements and the purpose of them is to give information about a given webpage to the search engines so that the engine can categorize them correctly.

Meta elements are inserted into the HTML document and are not visible to a user when he or she visits a site.

HTML

HTML (Hyper Text Mark up Language) is the language for web pages. It is written in the form of tags and surrounded by angle brackets.

XHTML

XHTML stands for Extensible Hyper Text Mark up Language. XHTML is the latest version of HTML and will gradually replace HTML.

CMS (Content Management System)

Content management system are becoming extremely popular these days simply because website owners does not have to learn about technical stuff or think about the coding of their websites rather they can focus all their energy into developing relevant content for their customers.

In fact in most of the content management system you do not have to write even a single HTML code.

Simply type in relevant information for Title, Keyword and other information at required places and coding is done by the CMS itself. Nowadays CMS is used not only by the small website owners rather even by big organizations.

Page Rank

Page Rank Technology was invented and developed by Google.

Page Rank of any web page on the internet reflects the view of Google that how importance is that particular web page.

Web page which Google believes are important receives a higher Page Rank and are more likely to appear at the top of the search results.

The concept behind Page Rank is that each "incoming link" to a "page A" is counted as a vote for "page A".

Google has a sophisticated technology to count these votes based on *quantity* and *quality* of the incoming links.

Page rank value varies from 0 to 10. Page rank of value 10 is of highest level of importance.

Google Toolbar

It is the excellent tool to see the page rank of any webpage on the internet.

Here you can see the *page rank of any webpage* in the Google tool bar (You have to put the curser for a moment to see the **actual** page rank).

Google toolbar has lots of other features. You can download the Google toolbar for Firefox from the following URL.

http://www.google.com/tools/firefox/toolbar/FT3/intl/en/index.html

Site map

The Sitemap allows you to inform the search engines about URLs on your websites that are available for crawling. By submitting a Sitemap to a search engine, you can help that search engine's crawlers to do a better job of crawling on your website.

Sitemaps are also beneficial for users particularly when users can't reach all areas of a website by following links.

URL (Uniform Resource Locator)

URL is the global address of documents and other resources on the World Wide Web.

The first part of the address is called a **protocol identifier** (for example it can be FTP or HTTP) and the second part is called a **resource name** and it specifies the **domain name** where the resource is located.

The protocol identifier and the resource name are separated by a **colon** and **two forward slashes**.

For example in the above example http://www.subodhgupta.co.uk

Here "**http**" is the **protocol** separated by ":" and two forward slash "**//**" and then finally **domain name** www.subodhgupta.co.uk

Anchor Text

It is an HTML text that links to another webpage or another location on the same page on the web.

Anchor text gives the website user a clear idea about the content of the destination page. Let's have a look in the following example:

<ahref="http://www.subodhgupta.co.uk/">**Subodh Gupta**</a>

The anchor text in the above example is **Subodh Gupta**

Inbound Link

An inbound link to your website from any other website is a link which is pointed towards your website.

For example if you have a website called www.peace.com and I have my website name www.subodhgupta.co.uk

Now if there is a link on my website which when I click will take me to your website www.peace.com, then it is an inbound link for your website and it is an outbound link from mine.

Outbound Links

Outbound links lower down the rank of a website. If your website ranks well, you may come across some "smart" webmaster asking you for a link exchange in a following way.

They would ask you to link their Main Website "say A" from your site and they in return would offer you to link to your site from their other less important website "say B" in order to improve ranking of their main "website A". Be watchful of these kinds of webmasters.

Link Popularity

The link popularity is one of the important parameter which webmasters use to improve the ranking of their website in the search engine results.

In general higher the Link popularity of a website the better will be its rank in the search engine results.

Link popularity of any website gives an indication to the search engine about the quantity and quality of other web sites that link to it.

The concept of link popularity of any website in the WWW is same as that of importance of any human being in the business world.

As more important the person is more people would know him, so in a similar way important site will attract many inbound links and hence high link popularity.

Poorer or less important is the person and less people want to know about him and in a similar way web sites with poor content or less important will have difficulty attracting any inbound links from other website.

Link Farm

Link farm are any group of web sites that link to one another with the main objective of increasing the link popularity of their website and hence the rank on the search engine results.

Link farms were developed by black hat search engine optimizers and are considered as unethical by search engine. Participation in link farm activity can leads to the banning of the website.

On Page Factors

On page factors are the website optimization factors on the organization or owner's own website which are under the control of their own webmaster.

As a general rule "on page" factors are less important for search engines as compared to "off page" factors simply because they are easy to manipulate by the webmasters.

However that does not mean that you should forget about them. You need to consider both the factors (on page and off page) in order to improve the ranking of your website in the search results.

The examples of on page factors are

(a) HTML page title

(b) Keywords

(c) Text content on the webpage

Off Page Factors

Off page factors are the website optimization factors which are not on the organization or owner own website.

The examples of off page factors are

(a) Numbers of inbound links

(b) Quality of inbound links

(c) Anchor text in the inbound links

Web Crawler

A web crawler (also known as a web spider or web robot) is an automated program which browses the World Wide Web. It accesses a web site and travel through it by following the links present on the web pages.

This process of browsing the World Wide Web by web crawler is called web crawling or spidering.

Directories

Directories are important because they provide the webmasters one way inbound link to improve the link popularities of their website. Over the period of time hundreds of web directories have grown up on the internet and many of them charge the money for registration for providing the inbound link. However not all the directories are worth for paid inclusions.

Two most important directories are DMOZ and Yahoo directories. DMOZ offers free inclusion of websites and provide listing for Google directory. It is also important because of its high Google Page Rank of 8.

http://www.dmoz.org/

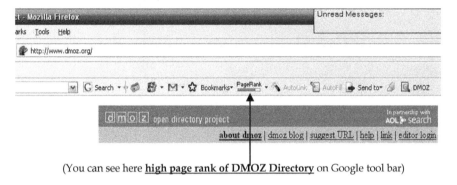

(You can see here **high page rank of DMOZ Directory** on Google tool bar)

Black hat SEO

Search Engine optimization methods which are considered as unethical by search engines.

These methods can lead to banning of the website from the search engine results.

These are used for manipulating the ranking of the website on search engine results.

Part 2

Search Engine Optimization

Each webpage in the website is analysed individually by the search engines.

Step 1

HTML Title

HTML text element is the most important text element *because it gets the maximum exposure in search engine results pages*.

Let's understand it with the help of an example. HTML page title **"in the code"** may look like:

<title> Vipassana Meditation Website </title>

Webpage with above **HTML title** would look like as

In the **search engine results pages, HTML title** would look like as follows

Vipassana Meditation Website
Homepage of the organization which offers **Vipassana Meditation** courses as taught by SN Goenka.
www.dhamma.org/ - 12k - Cached - Similar pages

So you can see in the above example that the *HTML text element* gets the maximum exposure in the search engine results i.e. it is the most important text elements.

I came across number of beautiful website but having major mistakes. The web designers may design beautiful website but not necessary that they are aware of your organization goal and objectives and often make mistake when writing the **page title.**

Always remember to include your main keywords in the HTML page title and also at the same time your title page should convey the main message.

You may need to write unique page title for each of your webpage and remember that the title tag should not be more than 65 characters long.

Many organizations who achieve good ranking on search engines sometimes still find few customers are converting to them or clicking their website. The main reason behind this is that they don't have compelling message for their customer in their HTML title page.

Remember: Your HTML title should be extremely focussed and compelling for each webpage as it is the most important text element and it will help you to improve the click through rate for your website in the search results.

Step 2

Web page Content

Write nicely drafted content for all your web pages as this is very important and step no 2 in my opinion for search engine optimization.

The text on your webpage should be relevant and should contain the targeted keywords where needed.

Following points must be considered when writing web pages for any website as they will help you to optimise your website for various search engines and at the same time helpful in good user experience.

(a)**HTML Text:** Remember that the whole process of web search is text based and search engines do care what text you have on your webpage. Here text means HTML text but not the graphical text because search engine can't read them.

(b)**Page size**: Bigger page size is the common mistake I have seen in various websites. Web designers put lots of images on web page to make it look beautiful but in turns make it very heavy.

Now even in country like the UK, not everybody has broadband i.e. the speed of the Internet will be slow in dial up connections.

So if the user has to wait for the long time for opening your website, the chances are that he or she may skip your website

Vipassana Meditatio
Homepage of the organiza
Goenka.
www.dhamma.org/ - 12k -

unless desperately looking for you. Personally I would suggest that page size should not be more than 40 KB and preferably about 10 to 15 KB.

You can check the size of any web pages on Google search results in front of URL.

For example you can see page size as **12 k** in front of the URL in the above Google search results.

Remember that web pages you made should be lighter in size so that user can open them easily without waiting for long time.

(c)**Length of webpage**: Webpage should not be too long and on the other side as a general rule there should be at least 200 words on the webpage. Around four hundreds words on each webpage are ideal.

(d)**PDF or excel files on webpage**: Preferably avoid PDF or other files on your website as it disrupt the user experience while surfing.

(e)Broken Link on webpage: Remember to check on your website that there should not be any broken link.

You can check broken link on web pages from the following website: **Link Checker**
http://validator.w3.org/checklink

(f)Fresh Content

Is information on your product or training service up to date?

Remember that search engines like websites with fresh content. So keep updating your website regularly.

With more and better content on your website your search engine visibility would improve because as a general rule, more pages means better ranking and more people would be happy to link to you however the pages should be of relevant content.

(g) Outgoing links

Keep the outgoing link from any webpage to other website into limit as outbound links lower down the rank of a webpage.

Fewer the outgoing links from any webpage the better the page rank will be. However that does not mean that there should not be any outgoing link rather they should be there only where needed.

Step 3

Keywords

Personally I think **keyword selection** is the most important decision in the Search engine optimization process because if the wrong keywords are selected then the whole of the SEO effort will be simply a waste and would result in a major revenue loss.

Your keywords should be based on your organization goals, your product and services and your target audience.

When deciding keywords, you should focus on your product or services and get into the shoes of your target audience and think what keywords you would type if you are searching for your kind of product or services.

After writing your keywords you can take a help from Google to find out what people are searching for your kind of product or services or you can get alternative keyword based on what consumer are searching.

It is extremely important that the keyword you choose should be the one which people on the internet are searching.

Google provides the excellent *keyword tool* which is based on actual user query used in Google adwords program.

https://adwords.google.com/select/KeywordToolExternal

Remember: Unless you do not focus on the relevant keywords which people are using, all your efforts of search engine optimization could be wasted.

You also need to consider if your products or services are more likely to be sold in one geographical region, as in that case it is best to have your keyword of "two words" or may be "three" rather than one single word.

For example if you provide Yoga classes in London, you should aim for keyword as "Yoga London" rather simply "Yoga".

There are 2 primarily reasons for this:

(a) It is more likely that a person sitting in London looking for yoga classes would type "Yoga London" or "yoga classes in London" rather than only typing "yoga" and you will get a more relevant customer.

(b) It is very difficult for a new website to compete on one single keyword word "yoga" with already existing websites or web portals as there will be much more competition for a keyword of "one word" rather than when you target on your niche area and compete on keyword which is of "two or three word" and which will also be more relevant to you. For example when you type keyword of <u>one word</u> say "Yoga"

More than 100 million results

You can see that there are more than 100 millions results for keyword of **one word** which makes it almost impossible for a new website to compete on keyword of **one word**.

However if you type keyword "Yoga London" made up of two words only which is also relevant to you.

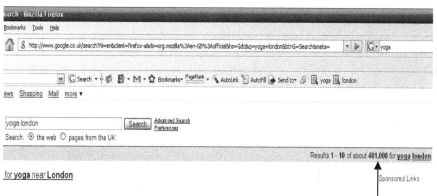

In this case you can notice, there are only about **half a million results.**

So for keyword of "one word" there are more than 100 millions results to compete with and for keyword of "two word" there are only about half a million result. So it is very clear that it is easy to compete on niche keywords.

Also you need to remember that if your website is not in the top 20 results for the selected keywords, it won't bring you many customers. In fact for regular flow of customers your website must be in top 10 results of search engines and that is easier to achieve if you are competing on niche keyword which are made up of "two or three words".

You may need to focus on different keywords for different pages on your website. For example your home page may be focused on your company name but other pages may be focussed on different keywords depending upon your products and services.

Remember: Keyword selection is the most important decision in your SEO campaign. I would suggest for a small or medium size website to focus on no more than 5 keywords or preferably 3 main keywords and 2 other of lesser importance unless you are running a big budget website for a MNC and you have to optimise 100's of keywords.

Once your keywords are decided, remember to put these keywords in your (a) HTML title page (b) Description title (c) Keyword tag (d) Of course while writing content for all your web pages wherever needed and make sure that you have adequate keyword density on all your web pages for the respective keywords.

What you should never do with the keywords

You should never do Keyword stuffing (excessive keywords on a webpage).

Some website owners, thinks that since keywords are very important for higher ranking of website so they try to load their web pages with excessive keywords in an attempt to manipulate a site's ranking in search engine results.

Some webmaster tries to hide the keywords in content of their web pages by using text of the same colour as the background of the webpage.

For example using white text on a white background of webpage thinking that it will be only visible for search engine and ranking can improve.

These kinds of practice can cause your site to be perceived as dodge by the search engines as it gives different information to search engines than their website visitors.

If you fill the webpage with lots of keywords, first it will results in a negative experience for your website visitor and then it can also harm your site's ranking as your website may get banned by search engines.

Remember your focus should be on creating useful content for your customer along with the relevant keywords where needed.

Always remember that there is no one single factor that can put your website on top rank.

It is the combination of various factors which helps your website to achieve better rank on search engine results.

Step 4

URL

It is very important that *your URL's should contain the targeted keywords* as this will help your website to get better ranking.

Let's have a look at the following two examples.

You would see in the following examples that in general for any targeted keyword, most of the top ranking website which will appear on page 1 will have the targeted keyword in their URL in the results of search engine results pages.

The keyword in the URL will also be highlighted in the search results pages which indicate the importance of the keyword in the URL.

Example 1: Keyword: Stock

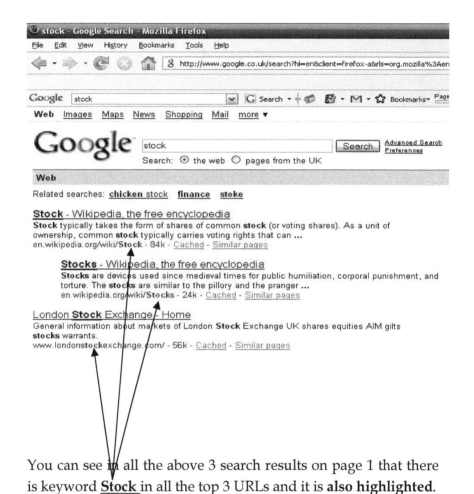

You can see in all the above 3 search results on page 1 that there is keyword **Stock** in all the top 3 URLs and it is **also highlighted**.

Example 2: Keywords: Peace

Again you can notice "keyword" **peace** in all the above 3 top ranking URL in the search results and it is **also highlighted**.

Step 5

Inbound Links

The inbound links are considered very important in the search engine algorithm because they are "off page factors" and cannot be influenced by the webmaster directly and at the same time indicate the page quality and popularity on the internet.

Steps to improve your inbound links and link popularity

(a) Submit your website to all the directories, **especially DMOZ which is Google page rank 8** and it is also free.

Normally all the business association or trade association have their website, if you are member of any one of them you can get a link to your website from your association.

You can also submit your website to niche directories which are specifically focussed on your product or services. Sometimes you need to pay for submitting your site.

However you also need to take into account the page rank of the webpage of the directory from which you would get the inbound link.

There is no much benefits to pay and get the link to your site if the page rank of the respective webpage is "zero" or "one" and have many outbound links are there from that webpage.

(b)When you launch your website or any new product or service, remember to distribute your press release online with a link to your website so as to get the extra inbound link.

(c)Write informative articles and submit them to article directories. If other website owner finds your article informative they would be happy to publish your articles on their website and in return they would link your website from their own website.

(d) You can request to websites which has similar content as that of your for link exchange, *if they are not your direct competitors*. However you need to remember that website to which you are writing for link exchange (even though having similar content) must be credible and not involved in selling or purchasing links.

You can easily find the number of inbound link to your website or to various web pages of your website at Yahoo Explorer **http://siteexplorer.search.yahoo.com/**

Yahoo Site Explorer is a very useful tool and with this help you can found total inbound link to the main page of your site or total inbound link to all the pages of your website and also allows you to explore all the web pages indexed by Yahoo! Search.

Yahoo Site Explorer

You need to put your website URL in *the explore URL search box* and simply with one single click it can show all the web pages indexed in the yahoo and also number of inbound links.

If you have prepared and submitted the Google sitemap (*which I would certainly recommend one should*) then in Google webmaster tools there is link section where you can easily see all the links both **inbound links** (pages with external links) and **internal links** within the website (pages with internal link).

Step 6

Anchor Text

Anchor text is still an important factor in search engine optimization process though its importance has come down in the last one year.

The anchor text is the visible, clickable text that a user would click on to follow a link. Anchor text gives indication about the content of the destination page to the user and as well as to the search engines i.e. it needs to be relevant.

The objective of search engines is to provide relevant search results to the user and anchor text helps into this process and this is the reason it is considered important.

Many website designers make mistake from the perspective of search engine optimization when they link the pages even within their own website. For example you might have a webpage about **"Drilling Machine"** on your site. What **text** do you think should be there in the **anchor text** when you link this page from other pages? Obviously **drilling machine**

Similarly there should be relevant keyword in the anchor text for linking to every other respective page on the World Wide Web isn't it?

Yes you are thinking right but reality is different. There are millions of **link** with the **anchor text** <u>Click here</u> on millions of website which are totally irrelevant to identify the content on the destination, ever thought why? Simply because many website designer still do not understand the importance of *anchor text* in the link and make a mistake.

Let's understand it further with the help of an example about the mistake which site designer do in the case of above keyword "drilling machine".

We have to link the web page which is about "**drilling machine**" from other web page and we have the following text content on the other webpage as follows in option (a) and (b).

(a) For more information about drilling machine please <u>click here</u>

(b) For more information about <u>drilling machine</u> please click here

In which of the above option the correct anchor text is used in the hyperlink?

Well the answer is of course option (b) but I still see many website designers even now make the same mistake again and again and put anchor text as <u>**click here**</u> in the hyper link.

Now it may be possible that somebody links to your site from his site and may not use the right anchor text however remember that at least you have the full control over the anchor text in the internal links within your own website so use it wisely.

Step 7

Age of a website

I think *age of a website and to some extent domain age also has some effect on the ranking of a website* on the search engine results and certainly taken into account by many search engines.

The reason for this is that it can't be faked. Let's have a look at one of the following example of a website.

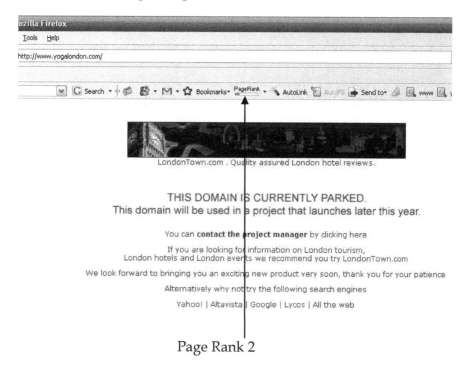

Page Rank 2

(a)This website www.yogalondon.com is of only one page and domain is still parked.

(b)It has only one inbound link that too from other webpage of Google page rank 3 which also has about 50 outgoing link i.e. the value of that inbound link cannot be good.

(c)This webpage has no content about yoga in London i.e. no keyword density in the content about keyword "Yoga London" and also no valuable text content for the users.

(d)The webpage has 10 outgoing link which further lower down the page rank of this webpage.

(e)It has HTML text in the page title **<title> Welcome to Yogalondon.com</title>** which certainly matches with URL http://www.yogalondon.com/ but does not have text content on webpage to match the text in HTML page title.

So in way this website example does not follow the rules or step for SEO which I have described above i.e. not following Step no 2 (content on webpage), step 3 (keyword on webpage), step no 5 (number of inbound links) as there is only one inbound link, however this webpage was still on page 1 in top ten ranking results of Google UK search results for the keyword **Yoga London** till couple of months before and it stayed there for about more than 6 months in year 2007.

It is not there now in the top 10 results anymore but the point I want to highlight is that **how did it attained ranking on top 10 results of Google? Interestingly it still has the Google page rank 2** which is difficult to get for any new website of even 50 webpage in the first 6 to 8 months even though follows most of the above steps.

The only reason which can explain all the above confusion is that *Google give importance to the age of website as this domain is aged and parked from a long time*. This domain was created on 12 Feb 2002.

So more than 6 years it has been parked which gives this page Google page rank 2 without doing any SEO efforts.

Anyhow since this webpage is not there on the top search results of Google on the keyword of "Yoga London" anymore, this shows that this factor of age has also been diluted by Google but since it still has the page rank of 2 which shows that it still matters though may be less.

Age of the website does matter in the ranking of a website in the search engine results.

Other useful steps for SEO

(a) Meta Description tag

Although less important than HTML page title tag as this is not displayed many times and it is not under your control when it will be displayed however needless to say that it should also be unique for each page as your HTML title page.

(b) Meta Keyword Tag

In this tag webmaster or the site owners can place their various keywords for the search engines however remember never to stuff the keywords.

This tag is also invisible and it is especially for the search engines. Since this tag is also under the control of webmaster it has less value in terms of ranking however needs to be considered carefully.

(c)Google Sitemap

Google sitemap is a special map only for the Google search engine and it is different than normal sitemap.

Although Google sitemap won't put your website on top ranking position in the search results by itself as its objective is to help webmaster or website owner to submit their websites URL directly to Google and more possibility to get their website pages indexed quickly into the Google index.

However for submitting your **Google sitemap** you need to sign up for **Google webmaster tool account** and once you sign for Google webmaster tool account you will find vital information into it about your website, example (a) Inbound links (b) internal links(c) Errors and problems encountered by Google's crawlers while accessing pages on your site (d)Indexed pages from your website into the Google index (e) top 20 keywords from which users reached your site and lots of other important information which is literally must if you really want to rank higher in the search engine results.

So in a way Google sitemap along with the Google webmaster tool account will help you to optimise your website and would help you to rank better in the Google search engine and in the other search engine as well as every search engine loves good practice and optimise website.

For submitting Google sitemap you need to perform few simple steps and the details is available on the following pages of Google.

What is a Sitemap file and why should I have one?
http://www.google.com/support/webmasters/bin/answer.py?answer=40318

How do I submit a Sitemap?
http://www.google.com/support/webmasters/bin/answer.py?answer=34575 &topic=13451

This service from Google is free and your website pages would be indexed faster in the Google once you submit the sitemap.

Do remember to make a sitemap of your website and submit it to the Google as it can help search engine robots to navigate easily.

SEO don'ts

Now that you have learnt what you need to do for SEO, *it is equally important to learn what you shouldn't do,* as otherwise website could be banned from the search results of major search engines.

Never link your website to a banned website.

Never purchase the links or participate in mass link exchange scheme.

Never do the *keywords stuffing* on the webpage of your website.

Never put the *hidden text* or hidden links on the website.

Never make *duplicate pages* on your website.

Never use images instead of text to display important names, content or links as the Google crawler doesn't recognize text contained in the images.

Never present different content to search engines than what you display to users (commonly referred as "cloaking").

Never use unauthorized computer programs to submit web pages, check rankings as these programs consume computing resources and violate the terms of service of Google.

Remember: Never invest too much time into any one aspect of SEO as you may end up ignoring others. The best is to take a holistic approach and focus on all the 7 main parameters.

Part 3

Recording and Measurement

This third and final part is about *recording* and *measuring the improvement* in the ranking of your website in the major search engine results. *It is very important because it will keep you motivated when you see the positive results.*

However you need to remember that it takes some time for the results to show up. For example search engine like Google generally update their index once in a month i.e. so give it some time to get your changes updated in its searched results. So if you need to check the increase in the number of pages indexed by Google, check after at least 4 weeks. However the process can become faster if you have submitted your sitemap to the Google.

Similarly after your optimization of your webpage, HTML title and keywords wait for about 4 to 6 weeks to see the changes in the ranking of your website on targeted keywords in the search engine results.

Building **inbound links** is the ongoing process and for Google page rank it can easily take even months or maybe even a year before page rank of a webpage improve from zero to three, so it would be a waste of time if you keep checking page rank of your various pages anytime in less than a month.

Before beginning your search engine optimization process, it is important that *first you should measure your present position of your website* on various parameters like (a) Number of indexed pages (b) Ranking of your website on your main keywords (c) Inbound link (d) Page rank of your main landing web pages, otherwise you would never know your improvement.

Remember: Check all the parameters or results of your SEO efforts only once in a month. Daily or weekly checking will be a waste of time.

Pages Indexed

Here you can record how many pages of your site are indexed in the various search engines.

For Google

	Today(date)	4 weeks	8 weeks	12 weeks
Number of Pages Indexed				

For Yahoo

	Today(date)	4 weeks	8 weeks	12 weeks
Number of Pages Indexed				

For MSN

	Today(date)	4 weeks	8 weeks	12 weeks
Number of Pages Indexed				

Keyword Ranking (in Google)

Keywords	Today	4 weeks	8 weeks	12 weeks

Keyword Ranking (in Yahoo)

Keywords	Today	4 weeks	8 weeks	12 weeks

Keyword Ranking (in MSN)

Keywords	Today	4 weeks	8 weeks	12 weeks

Inbound Links (in Google)

Home page URL

	Today	6 weeks	12 weeks	18 weeks
Number of inbound Links				

Landing page no 1 URL

	Today	6 weeks	12 weeks	18 weeks
Number of inbound Links				

Landing page no 2 URL

	Today	6 weeks	12 weeks	18 weeks
Number of inbound Links				

Inbound Links (in Yahoo)

Home page URL

	Today	6 weeks	12 weeks	18 weeks
Number of inbound Links				

Landing page no 1 URL

	Today	6 weeks	12 weeks	18 weeks
Number of inbound Links				

Landing page no 2 URL

	Today	6 weeks	12 weeks	18 weeks
Number of inbound Links				

Google Page Rank

Here you can record Google page rank of your 3 main landing pages in your website.

Home page URL ....

	Today(date)	4 months	8 months	12 months
Page Rank				

Landing page URL ....

	Today(date)	4 months	8 months	12 months
Page Rank				

Landing page URL ....

	Today(date)	4 months	8 months	12 months
Page Rank				

Number of Visitors

It is very important that you should also track number of visitors coming to your site every month. When your website ranking start improving because of search engine optimization efforts and you also optimise your content based on targeted keywords and make it compelling then number of visitors coming to your web site would also increase.

You can choose any tracking software which you find convenient for tracking the results. I would strongly recommend Google analytic, a free service offered by Google because it generates detailed statistics about the visitors to your website. If you are using Google adwords in that case it is already built in, alternatively you need to sign up with your Google account.

Date.....................

	During 1st Month	During 2nd Month	During 3rd Month
No of Visitors to your website after you begin your SEO process			

With consistent SEO effort you would see increase in the number of visitors to your website in the 2nd and 3rd month.

Useful websites

(1)Yahoo Search Blog
http://www.ysearchblog.com/

(2) Search Engine Marketing tip and News
http://www.searchenginewatch.com

(3)Link Checker
http://validator.w3.org/checklink

(4) Google webmaster central

http://www.google.com/webmasters/

(5) Google toolbar

http://www.google.com/tools/firefox/toolbar/FT3/intl/en/index.html

(6) Yahoo site explorer

http://siteexplorer.search.yahoo.com/

(7) Google Keyword tools

https://adwords.google.com/select/KeywordToolExternal

(8)Google Analytics

https://www.google.com/analytics/home/

Our Published Book

Understanding Indian Culture

&

Bridging the Communication Gap

"An inside journey to an Indian mind"

This is a practical book about bridging the communication gap between India and the West and understanding Indian culture.

This book will help you to understand what motivates Indians, how they negotiate, where they spend most of their money, what the younger Indian generation wants, etc.

It is based on real life experiences and will help you to understand Indians psychology which will make you more effective while doing business with Indians.

ISBN 978-0-9556882-5-6
Page 100 / Soft Cover / £14.95

For more details

Please visit our website: www.subodhgupta.co.uk

For any query related to bulk purchase please send us your email at:
info@subodhgupta.co.uk

All our books are also available at Amazon.co.uk, Barnes and Nobles

Doing Business in India and Understanding pitfalls

"The only book on understanding pitfalls while doing business in India"

This book focus in details on Indian real estate and retail market, BPO and IT industry, education system and examine some predictions on Indian economic growth by leading consulting organization.

This practical book will create awareness about business environment in India and certainly help you in avoiding the cost of expensive mistake.

This book is ideal for business leaders, managers or entrepreneurs from the West who are planning or already doing business in India.

ISBN 978-0-9556882-7-0
Page 156 / Soft Cover / £24.95

For more details

Please visit our website: www.subodhgupta.co.uk

For any query related to bulk purchase please send us your email at:
info@subodhgupta.co.uk

All our books are also available at Amazon.co.uk, Barnes and Nobles

Marketing Simplified

"Simple and a practical book on marketing"

This book will help self employed and small business owners to increase their profits and build up their businesses within a small budget.

This book will also help marketing managers working in a small and mid size organization to build a marketing plan step by step.

This book will help you to increase your sales and save your investment on the wasteful expenditure in various advertising campaign.

This book is also ideal for marketing students who want to understand marketing in a practical way.

ISBN 978-0-9556882-9-4

Page 68/Paperback/£4.95

For more details

Please visit our website: www.subodhgupta.co.uk

For any query related to bulk purchase please send us your email at:
info@subodhgupta.co.uk

Training workshops at workplace in London

We provide following workshops for corporate organizations in London.

(1)Understanding Indian Culture and Bridging the Communication gap.

(2)Doing Business in India and Understanding the Pitfalls.

(3)Half day Workshop on Work Life Balance.

(4)Half day workshop on (SEO) Search Engine Optimization

For more details please contact:

Barbara Tomasik
44(0)7966275913 (London) or info@subodhgupta.co.uk

Notes

Notes

Notes

www.ingramcontent.com/pod-product-compliance
Lightning Source LLC
Chambersburg PA
CBHW051214050326
40689CB00008B/1300